The Visit

A Collection of Poems

Virginia Balchin

Published by New Generation Publishing in 2021

First Edition

ISBN: 978-1-80031-378-1

www.newgeneration-publishing.com

New Generation Publishing

Poems by Virginia Balchin

Illustrations by Christine Maybank

Contents

Christmas Themed Poems

Poems on Christian Themes and Family Life

THE VISIT

The angel came
With wing and flame,

To Mary's home
Where she alone,

Was told the plan
From God for man,

You are the one
To bear My Son.

How can this be?

His mighty power
Will come this hour,

Bring heaven to earth
The Word to birth,

God chooses you
His work to do,

She bowed her head
"I will," she said,

With simple heart
She plays her part.

BEHOLD THIS MAN-CHILD

Wind - whining,
Cold biting,
Weary walking,
Pain fighting.

Jewish jostling,
Servants staring,
Courtyards closing,
Quiet despairing.

Night-time falling,
Donkey dragging,
Mary moaning,
Joseph flagging.

Sudden saving,
Inn-man's insight,
Stable opening,
For the birth-night.

Warming cowshed,
In the dim light,
See the crowning,
Of the birth fight.

Joseph weeping,
Mary sighing,
Holds the living,
Knows the dying.

Earth is silent.
Heaven is still,
Behold this man-child.
Does God's will

NEARLY READY - *thoughts of Mary?*

It's nearly ready
So beautifully made
Perfectly shaped, and
Softly smoothed.

So much time he has spent – my Joseph
Night after night by dimly lit oil lamp
Out in the darkening workshop
Making a crib for the child
Overshadowed himself
By a sense of awe
At the coming of the child
And so, it's nearly ready

Nearly ready - I'm nearly ready
Excited, frightened,
Seeing the impossible, growing daily.
So often wondering - is it really happening?

The overshadowing of God on me,
Bearing fruit -
Deep within.
Making a home for the child
Within my very self

THE INNKEEPER

"There is no room"- I said to him
Although I saw his cloak was thin;
His eyes were tired, his head went down,
"There is no room in all this town".

But as he turned to walk away,
I knew that I must let him stay,
For in his shadow-there she stood,
With head bowed low beneath her hood.

As she looked up, she gave a sigh-
Followed by a frantic cry.
"The child is coming -on His way
Oh, please sir; please sir, let us stay".

I stood confused-what could I do?
Then with a sudden start, I knew.
"There is my stable- that is all,
. Built into the rockface wall"

"I'll bring fresh hay and bedding too,
My wife will come and help you through".
They slowly walked into my cave
Poor they looked -but very brave.

And later when the guests were fed,
My weary travellers all in bed.
I stepped outside into the night
Surprised to find a new star's light.

My wife called out to me with joy,
"Oh come and see this special boy";
And as I bent at stable door
My heart was touched by sudden awe.

I peered inside and there she lay,
The baby cradled in the hay,
The man held up the child for me
Unwrapping him so I could see.

And as I looked into his face
I know I saw a perfect trace,
Of God come down into this place.

God in my inn this very day,
The child I nearly sent away.

Christmas 1996
"Hail the Incarnate Deity!"

THE WELCOME

No cozy cot-no knitted shawl
But prickly straw and oxen stall.

No nursery frieze and mobile bright
But chilling breeze and wintry night.

No greeting cards and gifts piled high
But secret signs across the sky.

No welcoming home, prepared and warm
But stable bleak; for kingly form.

And so, the earth, that precious day
Turned its back and looked away.

So, shall we, like innkeepers there,
Close the door, refuse to share?

Deny Him entrance to our life
Hold on to selfishness and strife?

Or shall we turn and face the King
Say - welcome home and come on in.

THE WELCOME (part 2)

We thank you Lord God
That, as a man, you chose to have
No home of your own
No wife alongside you
No earthly children to love you.

Lord come again this Christmas
To the homeless
To the lonely
And to the unloved.

Come again – through our hands
And through our hearts

CHRISTMAS IS ....

Christmas is - a last minute dash to the supermarket for a trolley load of goods to cram into an overstocked larder.

Christmas is – a long, weary five day walk to Bethlehem and nowhere to stay.

Christmas is - worrying whether there will be enough roast potatoes - and where's the cranberry sauce got to?

Christmas is - a desperate search for a room - a place - anywhere for Mary to lie down.

Christmas is - a frantic few minutes in the kitchen trying to get the Christmas pudding "out" in one piece!

Christmas is - a man and woman delivering a baby alone in a dirty stable.

Christmas is - a sea of wrapping paper and a multitude of expensive presents.

Christmas is - the gift of adoration in the eyes of a few rough shepherds.

Christmas is - crackers with plastic toys and paper hats round a laden tea-table.

Christmas is - gold, frankincense and myrrh - that foretell of a life of suffering and sacrifice.

ELIZABETH

This has been the strangest year.
Full of joy and tinged with fear,
"The barren one" has been my name
Full of sadness and of shame.

And despite our priestly call
We have no son; no child at all,
We've hoped and prayed but all in vain
No child to carry on the name.

And then one day the lot was cast,
My husband chosen for the task
Of entering the Holy place
To represent God's chosen race.

For many days I sat to wait
To hear his footsteps at the gate;
And then he came in from the night
His face and eyes so full of light.

I questioned but there was no sound,
A writing tablet soon was found.
He slowly wrote it down for me
And lifted it so I could see.

An angel in the Holy place
Spoke to me there with shining face
"God says that we will have a son,
To walk before His coming One."

But sadly, I did not believe
We are too old now to conceive
The angel said, "your son will come
Until that time, you will be dumb."

We held each other-then I knew
That what the angel said was true
My heart was flooded full with joy
To think that we would birth a boy.

For months at home, I hid away
Waiting for that special day
Then suddenly a tiny start
A quickening beneath my heart.

And very soon along the way
Came cousin Mary here to stay.
So pure so beautiful she stands
And reaching out she clasps my hands.

The child within leaps up with joy
He recognised the Saviour boy.
Blessed are you Mary -chosen one
To be the Bearer of God's son.

We sat and talked and laughed all day
So glad was I she came to stay
We knew the secret of God's plan
That He Himself would become man.

She left and soon my time had come
With pain and anguish came my son.
And later we called out with joy
That God had given us a boy.

What is his name the neighbours say
He must be named -be named today.
His father stood the room was stilled
He took a breath -his mouth was filled.

His name is John- it is God's will
He has a purpose to fulfil
For God's Messiah is on the way
John will prepare you for this day.

And as I held my child at last
A shadow over me was cast,
I knew his life was not for me
That it would pain and trouble see.

But I am glad to play a part
In all the love of God’s great heart.

HE CAME DOWN

From beyond time and space
Beyond imaginings
He came down

Passing flaming stars
Through interstellar space
He came down

Through the blackness of deep heaven
Past silent revolving planets
He came down

Through earth's shining atmosphere
And the clouds of night
He came down

Along draughty streets; through stable door
Into splintery stall
He came down

And unseen, unheard, uncomprehended
Glory settled on the child
He came down

But the angels, peering over the vault of heaven
Waited for the earth to erupt with rejoicing
At His coming

Amazed by earth's echoing silence; they took flight
A multitude of winged brightness,
To announce his coming
And yet He came down.

SHINING STAR

SHINING STAR
SINGING SERAPHIM
SILENT SHEEP
STUNNED SHEPHERDS
STONY STREETS
SHADOWY STABLE
STUFF STRAW
SWADDLED SAVIOUR
SINLESS SON
SELF-GIVING SPIRIT
SUFFERING SERVANT
SUBMITTING SACRIFICE
SUDDEN SON RISE
STRONG SURVIVOR
SOARING SOVEREIGN
SHINING STAR

THE BABE IN THE STRAW

Did you see the babe today?
Hidden by the door?
Did you leave Him in the cold?
On His bed of straw?

Did you see the babe today?
Behind the cupboard door?
Shut away within the dark
On His bed of straw?

Did you see the babe today?
On the Christmas tree?
Hidden away behind the lights
And the presents there for me?

Did you see the Babe today?
And rush to bring Him in?
To sit together by the fire
And gladly sing to Him?

Will we see the Babe this year?
Hidden or in view?
Shall we welcome Him today
To live with me and you?

THE HOPE OF HEAVEN

(Luke 2:51)
"And Mary pondered (treasured) all these things in her heart"

The glory of Gabriel giving the good news,
The just decision of Joseph bringing her joy,
The traumatic travel to Bethlehem - in time,
The breathtaking, body bruising birth,
The holding to her heart the Hope of Heaven,
The stunned shepherds, silent in the stable,
The magnificent Magi and the meaning of the myrrh,

Holding close to her heart the Hope of Heaven.

WORSHIP THE KING

A manger cot – a bed of straw
A draughty shed – a workman poor
A flickering lamp - a bloodstained robe
Hush in excitement – spinning globe.

A growing boy – a laugh – a shout
A mother's heart – a joy – a doubt
Inside the frame – a spirit rare
A spirit pure is growing there

See now a man, beside the stream
See through the cloud, the dove's white gleam
See him stride forth – anointed son
Hush spinning earth and hear this one.

A silent crowd – a quiet voice
A blind man sees, the deaf rejoice
A hungry throng with bread is filled
He speaks, and raging storm is stilled

A noisy mob – an angry cry
A wooden cross – a woman's sigh
A bloodstained back – a man alone
Hush now in horror, earth of stone

See on a hill- the outstretched form
The jeering crowd – the sudden storm
Hear that last cry, oh spirit rare
That at the end speaks love and care

But look with me and see the grave
A blaze of fire lights up the cave
The Prince of life is bound no more
Hush waiting earth, from shore to shore

Rings forth the song – the Lord is King
The Father smiles – the angels sing
For God who made the spinning globe
Came on to earth – in fleshly robe

That men who scorned and jeered and killed
Could with the love of God be filled.

And as the earth shall ever spin
So, then our hearts should ever sing
JESUS IS LORD – JESUS IS KING!

CARNIVAL JESUS 2000

Did you come to the carnival?
And walk with the Jesus bus?
He came 2000 years ago
And still he's here with us.

Did you come to the carnival?
And see the banners fly?
Caught by the wind, bright in the sun,
The children held them high.

Did you come to the carnival?
And hear the music play?
With lots of lively Jesus songs
We sang and danced that day.

Did you come to the carnival?
And feel the joy and fun?
Well maybe just by being there,
We touched the heart of someone.

CONKERS IN THE KITCHEN

Conkers in the kitchen, acorns in the sink;
Coloured pencils everywhere and hardly time to think;
What noisy, lively children - why can't they clear away?
But off they go in such a rush to start another day.

What a pile of ironing, shirts are such a bore,
And here comes the dog again with more mud on the floor.
What shall we have for tea Lord, we had fish yesterday,
And Lord there seems so much to do, where is the time to pray?

The carpets need another clean, the baby needs her tea,
Daddy will be coming home; where is the time for me,
To spend with you Lord?
Oh, and yet, I love this busy family,
And so, do you.

EASTER

Bearing their spices and shedding their tears,
Moving with silent step, checking their fears;

Dreading the guards and fearing the stone,
Trembling to think of the flesh and the bone;

But loving their master and willing to bring,
The oils and the spices to one who was king;

But with the first faint shreds of day,
They see no guards to bar the way;

The mighty stone is out of place,
Their frozen blood begins to race;

They move towards the opened tomb,
And fearful, peer in through the gloom;

Oh joyful message that they bear,
The master is no longer there;

Death could not hold him Jesus lives,
And to the world good news he gives;

Come run with us and share the song,
That death has triumphed over wrong.

HE CAME IN THE LIKENESS OF MEN

He came in the likeness of men
He came in the likeness of men
And emptied Himself of the riches of heaven
He came in the likeness of men

He took up the towel to serve
He took up the towel to serve
And emptied Himself of the riches of heaven
He took up the towel to serve

He walked in obedience to death
He walked in obedience to death
And emptied Himself of the riches of heaven
He walked in obedience to death

And now He's exalted on high
And now He's exalted on high
Knowing again all the riches of heaven
For now He's exalted on high

Our tongues shall confess Him as Lord
Our tongues shall confess Him as Lord
For He gives unto us all the riches of heaven
Our tongues shall confess Him as Lord

CULTIVATING OUR LIFE PLOT.

Parable of the seeds: Luke 8

Planning

Clearing the ground

Planting the seed

Watering

Weeding

Supporting

Pruning

Harvesting

DANCE

I've found a joy, oh such a joy I know the Lord is in it
For He has opened up the way
Enabled me to reach and say
This is the feeling that I have
For Jesus' life has made me glad

And so, I reach out arms to You
My hands stretch up for blessing new
And in the movement
Up and high
I lose myself, touch the sky
I know my Lord is really there
I feel His love, His peace, His care.

Why should this be-I do not know
Why moving helps my praise to flow
And yet it does, and looking round
Faces reveal the joy they've found
And as we move in one accord
We symbolize your oneness Lord

LIVING IN LIFE

Not in death, nor in dusk,
Not in half-light, but day,
Come out of the shadows.
And live life this way.

Living in Life
In the Life of the Son
Of the crucified one
Hallelujah - in Life

Oh live in the flow
In the outpouring flow
Of the crystal of God,
Hallelujah - come low.

Oh live in the stream
In the stream of His Love
In the down of the Dove
Hallelujah - come in

Come wade in the stream
Come deeper, come deep
Till the waters can take you
Released in the sweep
Hallelujah, defeat!

Now rest in the current
Relax in His will.
And you shall go His way.
Hallelujah – the thrill

OBEDIENCE

Day after day I talked with them, till their minds burned with life
Through the living scriptures.
And my love for the Father hurt my earthly parents -
They did not understand
So, I became obedient unto them

But John knew me - he recognized God's lamb,
And to fulfil all righteousness
I was washed in the Jordan –
Identified with sinners
In glad obedience to the Father who wished it.
And in so doing it brought Father joy and the Spirit overshadowed me.

In the garden it was dark and cold and lonely.
No one understood, no one felt the pain inside my shrinking form,
The slow death - the humiliation,
The silent submission - which Father needed.

And then the cross - not even I could have known the worst pain of all - the total aloneness - the Father withdrawn, the Spirit removed,
Me alone with sin.
As my heart broke - God's love and righteousness poured out
In a mighty and ever-ongoing flood to me.
And Father held me close

RAINBOW

Rainbow - precious sign of love
Arching in the sky above,
Covenant with sinful man -
Heaven and earth touch in its span.

First the Light shines from the Lord –
Shines upon His Living Word –
Through the prism of His Son
Colours stream out - seven in one.

Red - the blood of God's own Son,
Forgiveness bought - salvation won;
Red that touches heaven above –
With arms spread out in deepest love.

Orange colour of the flame
Holy Spirit is His Name,
Burning up the dross and sin
That God's power may enter in.

Gold the splendour of the Son
Revealed through blood and flame, the one
Who stoops from heaven's highest place
To shine upon our upturned face.

Green for life - the plant, the tree
Springing fresh from earth for me,
Dependent on the sun and rain,
Creation's growth through joy and pain.

Blue the peace of Heaven's span
Over-arching every man –
Calling us to look above
To see God's purity and love.

Indigo - the King's dark robe –
Jesus sovereign of the globe –
Now in priestly robe He pleads,
Intercessor for our needs.

Violet - the fruitful vine -
Crushed to give the sparkling wine,
Bubbling new life - flowing free –
Rejoicing all who live in Thee.

Colours of the Rainbow – span
Come together in one man
Merge to form one shining Light
Crystal clear and dazzling white.

Jesus, precious Son of love,
Reigning in the Heavens above,
Reaching out to every place,
God's new covenant of grace.

RED LEAF

Green leaf, yellow leaf, red leaf- brown,
Down you tumble, down and down
From the oak tree dark and tall
See it swirling- falling – fall.

Mushy brown leaves line the ground,
Heavy boots then crunch and pound,
The single leaf is torn apart.
In death there is no work of art.

But see beneath the sodden earth
There comes a tiny sound of birth:
A shell has cracked, a root unfurls,
A shoot appears, a life uncurls,

For, safe beneath the leafy quilt
An acorn cup was warmed and split.
A life came forth where all seemed dead,
A shoot pushed up and raised its head.

A green leaf once came to the earth,
Perfectly veined, it came to birth.
A red leaf then hung from the tree
And fell to earth for you and me,

But that red leaf it cannot die
But lives forever in the sky
And new life swells where it lay dead
For from the wounds its sons are fed.

green leaf, yellow leaf, red leaf ~ brown, down they tumble, down and down...
G.B. Nov. 79.

REVERSAL

Thank you, Lord, for pangs of sadness,
Disappointment - just now broken in -
For as I look beneath the surface
I see wrong motives and the taint of sin.

Hopes and aspirations now seem shattered.
That which might have been - just will not be;
But it has made me cry in depth to Jesus
That He might touch the hurt and set me free.

Free from wrong desires and misplaced motives
Free from wanting what was not His plan
Free to really want what He has purposed
To create for God a useful, wholesome man.

For cleverness will last but for a lifetime
And brilliance can bring evil plans to birth -
But faith will last beyond our earthbound vision –
And hope can grasp what life is truly worth.

For what will really please our Heavenly Father
Is a heart that trusts and rests in Jesus' love
And in that love becomes a Jesus "carrier"
Directing others to a life above.

So, thank you for these bitter-sweet experiences
For through the tears we open up to You,
To get our wants in line with Father's life-plan
To start again with aspirations new.

STEPS

Tiny fingers reaching out, reaching for the table,
Can I reach it in one go - am I really able?
If I let go will I fall or will I make the edge?
Yes, I can, I'm sure I can- there I've made the ledge.

Small feet pushing hard - why won't the wheels go round?
If I can only make it go, I'll zoom across the ground,
Come on pedal, round you go, I'm pedaling very fast,
There it goes - I'm on the move - I'm riding it at last!

Splashing arms and kicking feet - why can't I get along?
Why can't I stay afloat today - where am I going wrong?
If I can only make the end, I'll get a badge for swimming,
Yes - there we are, I've done it now although my head is spinning.

And so, the child becomes a man,
Can stand upon his feet,
Can do so many clever things,
And every challenge meet.

But then one day God said to him
"Can you reach across to me,
By struggling can you get to heaven
My precious Son to see?"

"You reached the table as a babe,
The pedals turned at last,
You swam across the swimming pool,
And then your life moved fast".

"But no-one comes to me himself,
By struggling and by striving".
"I'm helpless ", said the man at last,
"My whole life I've been driving".

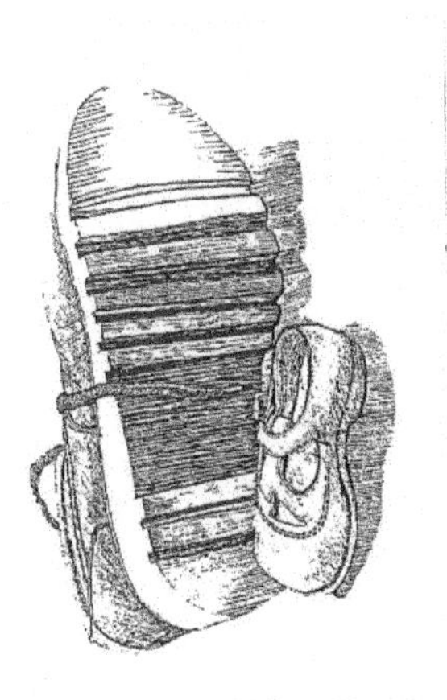

TAPESTRY

A canvas framework, rough and bare
Interlacing spaces there -
Nothing stands upon the frame
That will glorify His Name.
Look and see a coloured strand
Selected by a caring hand
See the strand is threaded in
Now the craftsman can begin.

Across the frame the colours spread
Dancing in the needle's head
Moved by His hand, each fills the space
And rests in its allotted space.

The pattern forms - stands out, is done
The colours blend - reveal the Son
Oh, Maker look upon the frame
A work to glorify Your Name.

A precious plan, a great design
Is woven by your life and mine
If we will - like the threaded strand
Be yielded in the Maker's hand.

THE ALABASTER BOX

She stood outside the door,
Trembling,
Wanting to knock,
Fearful to enter.

She clutched the box
Her treasure;
Such fragrance,
And recalled
The months of saving,
Eating little,
Buying nothing,
Until at last,
Enough.

She remembered those first glimpses
Of his face.
So strong - so gentle,
So at peace within.
A different face
A man among men
And she had known so many.
She had watched
When he touched the children,
Loving them for themselves;
Had seen him hold a leper;
Talk to a crowd,
Loving them and willing them
To understand and see beyond.

And now was her time
She ran across the room
And stood

The noise ceased
The heads turned

Silence fell
Fearful she searched the room
With her eyes
Until they met his
So peaceful – waiting for her
He stretched out a hand
She ran to him
In a moment
The box was broken

The ointment spilt
The fragrance rose
She buried her face
At his feet
Weeping
At that moment
She saw herself
Ugly, wounded, unclean
And longed to wash away
Her stain from his feet.

He knew her heart
Wrung with remorse
Longing for a new start
Then his hand touched hers
She looked up
And with his eyes
He met her need
Accepted, believed in her
Loved her as none other

And in his face
She saw herself
As herself
As he saw her
Renewed, pure, loving, forgiven

And she worshipped

THE KING'S GARLAND

Tall I stand, beautiful - alone.

My petals open one by one,
My heart stands out to feel the sun,
The need for budded scales is done,
The struggle to be formed is won.

My nectar stores are rich and sweet,
My pollen dusts the insects' feet,
My petals shine as silken sheets,
All things prepared - the day to greet.

But gripping hand and sharpened blade,
Come to destroy all that is made,
I'm lifted from my earthen bed –
My beauty can no more be fed.

What cruel hand has caused this blow?
That no more I can bloom and grow –
What senseless waste - untimely end –
Never again to sway and bend -

But others now are in His arm,
He seems to love us, seeks no harm –
And placed upon a table bare,
He starts a work of greatest care -

Each one He holds before His eyes,
·He notes our colour, shape and size,
A pattern He has in His mind,
The flower for every space to find.

And so, each bloom is intertwined,
With gentle touch; we twist and bind.
Each blossom makes its neighbour shine -
And no-one says 'the glory's mine'.

A garland of most perfect skill,
Each bloom is glad its place to fill,
And yet there comes a greater thrill –
A higher purpose to fulfil -

We have been picked to greet the King,
Our death is now a little thing,
Oh flowers look up to sigh and sing,
And celebrate this wondrous thing -

Our Maker's Son is coming -

We garland Him who comes to reign,
Great now our joy-that we were slain.

THE LINK PERSON

Oh Lord - I've come to tell you that I'm worried
I'm worried about him and anxious inside
I know he's facing a problem - I know it will hurt
And my heart goes out in anxiety over it
Yet I know I shouldn't be troubled.
While I trust in you - and so
I'm on my knees telling you about it
And you show me the three of us, holding hands
There you are - strong and tall - holding mine
And me, on my knees holding his
And in a moment I see what you are saying.

As I put my hand in yours and hold his
So your strength and your peace can flow
Through me to him - how amazing!
And I see too, how important it is
To keep tight hold of your hand
Because if I let go and hold only his
The power cannot get through
And if I hold only your hand
Releasing his, then
The strength stops short
So keep me in the middle
A link person.

THIS MOMENT

This morning at the kitchen sink,
With knife in hand - I stopped to think,
A sudden joy came sweeping in,
This moment - heart rose up to sing.

What caused this sweet unbidden joy?
What lifted self from its employ?
To gaze across the grass and trees,
And know that life was more than these?

Was it God's spirit's touch on me?
To lift my heart to worship thee?
To know there is a realm above,
Where all is sweet and all is love.

The moment passed - the work goes on,
But left behind there is a song,
For right beside the kitchen sink,
My soul with Jesus had a link.

THOMAS

Thomas - we have seen Him - we have seen the Lord.

I don't believe, I won't believe; - dead men cannot rise,
Unless I see the nail prints, I shan't believe your lies.

Thomas- we have seen Him - can't you feel our joy.

I don't believe, I won't believe; - I didn't see Him there,
Unless I feel the spear wound, your joy I cannot share.

Thomas - we have seen Him - we all received His peace.

I don't believe, I won't believe –
You've surely seen a ghost,
Unless I touch his flesh and bone - yours is an idle boast.

Thomas Thomas - turn around, turn around and look.

My Lord, my God - My Lord, my God, forgive my
doubting heart,
My Lord, my God - I do believe - give me another start.

TIDES

And the tide went out at Christmas
Exposing dread news, deep shock, dark moments
A clinging together in fear at the uncertainty
Then soon, soon a steady inflow again
Of God's grace, of God's love into our souls
A resurgence of faith in a God who knows
A belief that all this – must have purpose
A restoration of peace to heart and mind
Trusting again in the Lord – our shelter –
And soon – soon the tide will come in
Sweeping over the ugliness and rockiness
of the last few months
And we shall begin to forget.

And soon – very soon I shall be well
Pottering in the garden – tending the flowers
Making the meal and awaiting your return

So high tide will come again
A full sweep of life flowing between us
But a learning through it all that things are but passing
It's loving and being loved and Being that are Eternal.

TABLES

WRITTEN ON THE FLIGHT OUT OF CAPETOWN

Table of stone,
Towering over
The troubled townships.

Table of cloud,
Transitional between
Earth and heaven.

Table of the LORD
Towering over time
Transitional between
God and man

Transitory though I am
Come to my small table
Talk with me.

www.ingramcontent.com/pod-product-compliance
Ingram Content Group UK Ltd.
Pitfield, Milton Keynes, MK11 3LW, UK
UKHW020416250726
13967UKWH00007B/2664

9 781800 313781